A book created by
Michèle Fischhaber & Patrick Chernus

© 2017
What I Like LLC

Published by What I Like LLC
Zurich, Switzerland

© 2017 by What I Like LLC

All rights reserved. No part of this publication may be reproduced, stored in a retrieval system, or transmitted, in any form or by any means, electronic, mechanical, photocopying, recording or otherwise, without prior written permission from What I Like LLC.

ISBN 978-3-9524809-1-5

For custom or branded editions and corporate purchases please contact What I Like LLC at mail@whatilike.com

Written by Patrick Chernus & Michèle Fischhaber.

A big Thank You (*please check both*)
( ) to everybody who helped us to make this book happen
( ) to everybody who doubted and thought this would never work

What do you like?

What I Like

Content

Foreword — 7
About You — 8
Recent Stuff — 10
Places — 12
At Home — 16
Out & About — 19
Fashion — 20
Flea Market — 26
Pets & Other Animals — 27
Looking Good — 28
Senses — 33
Food & Beverage — 34
Sharing Stuff — 40
Generous vs. Stingy — 41
Art — 42
10 Things making you happy — 45
Music — 46
Sports — 50
People — 53
Movies & TV — 54
Colors — 57
Transportation — 58
Online — 62
Books — 66
Happy Ending — 70

What I Like™

Foreword

Hi,
you are holding *What I Like* in your hands. Congratulations! Do you always know what you want and what you like? If yes, good for you! However for most people that's not the case. Today offers so many choices that we lose track of what we really like. This inspired us to write this book.
We are Michèle and Patrick, the authors of *What I Like* – A question book about all your favorites. Starting with how you like your coffee, your all-time favorite places and what you like about your best friend.

With this book you'll (*please check all*)
( ) discover your all-time favorite things.
( ) remember what you liked as a child.
( ) be surprised how much you resemble your parents.
( ) realize what you admire about others.
( ) find out what matters and what doesn't.

When we started writing this book we shared the same sense of humor, from time to time a bottle of wine and a hunch that *What I Like* would change our lives. After countless nights of creating- and answering questions we learned so much about each other that we fell in love. So today we share a cat, a dog, a household as well as a small company which publishes the *What I Like books* worldwide.
We hope you'll enjoy this book as much as we did when we wrote it. Please feel free to fill it in or read out loud to your cat, your dog or other best friend.

Yours, Michèle & Patrick

About You

Three things you like about yourself (*don't be shy*)

1. _____

2. _____

3. _____

You love your mother for

(*this*) _____

You love your father for

(*this*) _____

The advantage of having a sibling:

(*this*) _____

The advantage of having you as a best friend:

(*this*) _____

Your most underestimated virtue:

(*this*) _____

Among other things you like to obsess on

(this) _____

In who's shoes would you like
to be in right now?

(in this person's shoes) _____

_____

You like your height.
( ) Yes   ( ) No

You like your weight.
( ) Yes   ( ) Your scale is usually exaggerating

You like your shoe size.
( ) Yes   ( ) No

You like your feet.
( ) Yes   ( ) No!

You like the way you are.
( ) Yes   ( ) No

Recent Stuff

The last thing you bought and loved:

(this thing) _____

The last thing you bought and got rid of soon after:

(this thing) _____

A recent find:

(this thing) _____

The last meal which impressed you was

at *(here)* _____

A song you remember whistling lately:

(song) _____

The last song you heard and downloaded right away:

(this song) _____

A book on your bedside table:

(this book) _____

Your last vacation was in

(this city / place) _____

(this country) _____

You spent your last day off mainly doing
( ) absolutely nothing.

( ) *(this)* _____

The last time you did something for the first time:

(this) _____

The last present you got from your mother:

(this present) _____

The last time you felt truly grateful:

(this) _____

Where you like to go

Places

What's your all-time favorite place in the whole wide world?

(this place) _____

(in / near this city) _____

(in this country) _____

( ) The internet

It's
( ) where you used to live.
( ) where you went on vacation.
( ) where you want to be.

Your first favorite place as a child was

(this place) _____

in / near *(this city)* _____

in *(this country)* _____

Your home is... *(please choose one)*
( ) where your parents live.
( ) where your team is.
( ) where your fridge is.
( ) where your chaos rules.
( ) where your heart is.
( ) where your sweetheart is.

Your all-time favorite country:

(this country) _____

Why? _____

_____

Your favorite city:

(this city) _____

Why? _____

_____

Your favorite street:

(name) _____

Your favorite park:

(name) _____

Your favorite river:

(name) _____

Your favorite lake:

(name) _____

Your favorite montain:

(name) _____

Your favorite valley:

(name) _____

Your favorite ocean:

(name) _____

Your favorite island:

(name) _____

Your favorite beach:

(name) _____

Your favorite secret escape:

(this) _____

Why? _____

_____

Living & Being

At home

What's your favorite piece of furniture at home?

(this piece) _____

It looks
( ) awesome.
( ) classy.
( ) like it was made for you.

What's your favorite room at home?

(this) _____

Your interior decorating style could be best dscribed as
( ) elegant shabby chic meets bourgeois bohème.
( ) random crapola.
( ) undefinable.

You couldn't help adopting your parent's taste.
( ) No way!
( ) Actually yes

Your mom's strategy to make you clean your room:
( ) Cold war
( ) Warm reminders
( ) Hot debates

As a child, you liked your room
( ) spic & span.
( ) jammed with toys.
( ) pink & cute.

Today, you live in
( ) a house.
( ) an apartment.
( ) a tent.
( ) your friend's car.
( ) your castle.

(or here) _____

You dream of living
( ) on a farm.
( ) in a big townhouse.
( ) in an RV.
( ) in a single family home.
( ) in a penthouse.
( ) in a treehouse.

(or here) _____

You like decorating your home
( ) for yourself.
( ) for your guests.
( ) for your pet(s).
( ) for your parents.

The last piece of furniture you bought and loved was

(piece) _____

(material) _____

( ) People find furniture   ( ) Furniture finds people

Out & About

Your first favorite place to go out:

(this club or venue) _____

in / near *(this city)* _____

Today, you enjoy going out to this place:

(this club or venue) _____

in / near *(this city)* _____

Your favorite restaurant as a child:

(this restaurant) _____

in *(this city)* _____

You liked going there
( ) because of the food. ( ) because of the nice waiters.
( ) because they had a playground you enjoyed.

Your favorite restaurant at the moment:

(this restaurant) _____

in *(this city)* _____

You like going there
( ) because of the food. ( ) because of the cute waiters.
( ) because of the crowd that goes there.

What you like to wear

Fashion

As you are holding this book in your hands
you are wearing

(this) _____

(this) _____

(and this) _____

( ) You look good!

What's your all-time favorite piece
in your closet?

(this) _____

in *(color)* _____

It's
( ) something you wear often.   ( ) too small.
( ) for special occasions only.

The age when you first became aware
there was something called fashion:

(age) _____

A fashion brand you remember from your childhood:

(this) _____

When you feel *(fill in each)*

happy, you wear _____

sad, you wear _____

angry, you wear _____

like making love, you wear _____

in love, you wear _____

staying in, you wear _____

naked, you wear _____

free, you wear _____

hot, you wear _____

nothing at all, you wear _____

You usually dress
( ) for yourself.
( ) for others.
( ) according to your mood.

Judging people by how they dress is
( ) superficial. ( ) super smart. ( ) superfluous.

Your personal style signifier:

(name) _____

When you meet another person, you first notice

(this) _____

From a fashion point of view - if you could go back in time you would love to live in

the (this era) _____

Your favorite pair of shoes:

(this) _____

(color) _____

( ) You own them   ( ) They own you

As a child it was tough to be in your shoes.
( ) Kind of
( ) Obviously they were too small for everyone else

The last pair of shoes you bought and loved:

(brand) _____

(color) _____

Shoe-perhero: This person has by far the best taste in shoes:

(this person) _____

Your favorite accessory:

(this) _____

Your favorite bag:

(this) _____

The first pair of sunglasses you bought, loved and lost:

(brand) _____

They were
( ) such a great deal!   ( ) expensive!   ( ) 2q24get

You hate belts.
( ) Yes   ( ) No

You wear hats
( ) on a bad hair day.
( ) for good inventions.
( ) to a horse race.
( ) just because!

Your favorit piece of jewelry:

(this) _____

You wear it
( ) all the time.   ( ) on special occasions only.

You wouldn't mind owning this watch:

(this) _____

from (year) _____

If you see something you like, you
( ) buy it. ( ) you think about it.
( ) you think about who could buy it for you.

If you see something you like
but it doesn't come in your size, you
( ) buy it one size smaller and skip dinner.
( ) buy it one size bigger and live in denial.

What's your favorite store right now?

(this) _____

Your favorite online store:

www. _____

Which one are you?
( ) You know what you want and where to find it.
( ) You never find what you are looking for.
( ) You always find what you don't need.

Flea Market

You like to get rid of things.
( ) True   ( ) False

Of all things you should finally get rid of this:

(this) _____

Five things you haven't been using for at least five years:

(this) _____

(this) _____

(this) _____

(this) _____

(and this) _____

You prefer buying this used:

(this) _____

Your best find ever:

(this) _____

You regret buying

(this) _____

Pets & Other Animals

Your favorite pet as a child:

(this) _____

A wild animal you would have loved to have as a pet:

(this) _____

Your favorite small animal:

(this) _____

Your favorite big animal:

(this) _____

Your favorite dangerous animal:

(this) _____

Best pet name ever:

(this) _____

If you were an animal you would be

(this) _____

Mirror, Mirror ...

Looking Good

What's your all-time favorite beauty product?

(product) _____

(brand) _____

It makes you
( ) feel younger. ( ) look good. ( ) smell good.
( ) less wrinkled. ( ) less pimpled.

You learned about baby skin while you were still a baby
( ) Yes ( ) No

Of all your parent's beauty products
this smelled by far the best:

(product) _____

(brand) _____

The last compliment you received for your hair was from

(this person) _____

Your favorite hairdresser?

(this person) _____

Your preferred hairdresser rhythm:
( ) Once a month ( ) Once a week ( ) Once a day

You have no problem leaving the house without shaving.
( ) Yes   ( ) No!

You like waxing
( ) your legs.   ( ) your face.
( ) restricted areas.   ( ) your skis.

If money didn't matter you would
( ) hire your own glam squad.
( ) bathe in donkey milk.
( ) use Champagne instead of shampoo.
( ) get a moneycure.
( ) not mind.

You enjoy hiring people who work on your body.
( ) Yes!   ( ) No!

This is okay to fake: (choose as many as you like):
( ) Tan
( ) Teeth
( ) Hair
( ) Monthly income
( ) ID
( ) Weight

You want to lose weight.
( ) Wait!   ( ) Who wouldn't?   ( ) You shouldn't

You like how your butt looks.
( ) Yes, but ...   ( ) Never saw it

Your essentials, because you're worth it *(check and fill in)*:

( ) Shower gel: _____

( ) Shampoo / Conditioner: _____

( ) Soap: _____

( ) Toothpaste: _____

( ) Shaving: _____

( ) Hair styling: _____

( ) Face cream: _____

( ) Body lotion: _____

( ) Deodorant: _____

( ) Perfume: _____

( ) Other: _____

( ) Makeup: _____

You love creating lists!
( ) So true!
( ) No

Looking in the mirror, this is your favorite feature:

(this) _____

A physical feature you are most complimented for:

(this) _____

The most beautiful person you know (from the outside):

(this person) _____

The most beautiful person you know (from the inside):

(this person) _____

Senses

Your top 3 favorite scents:

1. _____

2. _____

3. _____

Your favorite thing to touch:

(this) _____

Your favorite thing to look at:

(this) _____

Your favorite taste:
( ) sweet
( ) sour
( ) salty
( ) bitter
( ) umami

Your top 3 favorite sounds:

1. _____

2. _____

3. _____

What you like to eat and drink

Food & Beverage

Your perfect three-course meal:

(appetizer) _____

(main course) _____

_____

(dessert) _____

Your favorite beverages:

(non-alcoholic) _____

(alcoholic) _____

Your favorite beverage as a child:

(this) _____

Your favorite food as a child:

(this) _____

Your mother was an excellent cook.
( ) She was Jenny Oliver   ( ) She tried
( ) You chose to eat out   ( ) She had reservations about it

Back then, this vegetable was tolerable:

(this) _____

Today you prefer your veggies
( ) raw.   ( ) stir-fried.   ( ) frozen.   ( ) as French-Fries.

Your favorite fruit:

(this) _____

Your favorite meal of the day:
( ) Breakfast
( ) Brunch
( ) Lunch
( ) Dinner
( ) Dessert
( ) Snacks

Your favorite genre of food (*pick as many as you like*):
( ) Organic   ( ) Vegetarian   ( ) Vegan   ( ) Fast
( ) Ethnic   ( ) Soul   ( ) Asian   ( ) Local   ( ) Italian
( ) Home made   ( ) Delivered

( ) Other, like _____

This is how you like your eggs:
( ) Sunny side up   ( ) Poached   ( ) Hard boiled   ( ) Soft boiled
( ) Scrambled   ( ) You prefer them as Eggnog

Nutrition and you:
( ) You eat what you are
( ) You are what you eat
( ) You eat more than you want
( ) You want more than you eat

When you feel *(fill in each)*

hungry, you eat _____

angry, you drink _____

bored, you eat _____

sad, you drink _____

in love, you eat _____

intimidated, you drink _____

guilty, you eat _____

shameful, you drink _____

like eating, you eat _____

celebrating, you drink _____

happy, you eat _____

You are probably hungry by now, right?
The next thing you'll eat:

(this snack) _____

When you crave you crave
( ) junk food. ( ) health food. ( ) BACON!!!

You count calories.
( ) Yes ( ) No

You eat carbs.
( ) Yes ( ) No

You try to eat fat free.
( ) Yes ( ) No

You like sweets.
( ) Yes ( ) Yes ( ) Yes ( ) Yes ( ) Yes ( ) Yes

You usually cook
( ) for yourself. ( ) for other people. ( ) never.

When you cook for other people
( ) you tend to cook way too much.
( ) you are afraid of not having enough.
( ) you get food delivered.

When you cook for yourself, you get your groceries
( ) directly from the farmer. ( ) from the convenience store.
( ) online. ( ) from your own backyard.
( ) from the neighbors backyard. ( ) You don't cook. Ever.

When there's nothing in the fridge,
you most likely order

(this) _____

Your preferred fast food chain:

(this chain) _____

After eating there you tend to feel
( ) sick.   ( ) full.   ( ) satisfied.   ( ) like you want more.

Your favorite coffee shop:

(this coffee shop) _____

You take your coffee
( ) black.   ( ) with cream & sugar.   ( ) to go.   ( ) iced.

( ) Actually, you prefer tea.

The cherry on top – Your absolute favorite dessert:

(this) _____

_____

You always have room for dessert.
( ) Yes

Sharing Stuff

Which one is it? Or is it both?
( ) You like to share with other people
( ) Other people like to share with you

You most likely share (*pick one*)
( ) your car.
( ) your clothes.
( ) a secret.
( ) knowledge.
( ) good advice.
( ) tips.
( ) funny videos.
( ) your friends.

( ) You don't share food!!

Those who share are those who care.
( ) True ( ) False

With this person you would share everything:

(this person) _____

With this person you would share absolutely nothing:

(this person) _____

You are comfortable to share feelings with

(this friend) _____

Generous vs. Stingy

The most generous person you know and love:

(first name) _____

(last name) _____

The stingiest person you know and like:

(first name) _____

(last name) _____

You are most generous with this friend:

(first name) _____

(last name) _____

You are most generous with
( ) food.
( ) your car.
( ) clothes.
( ) your friends.
( ) your parents.

Sometimes you are a bit stingy

with *(this little thing)* _____

Like it or not

Art

Your all-time favorite piece of art:

(title) _____

_____

by *(artist)* _____

( ) You own it and it's on your wall
( ) You own a poster print of it
( ) If you spent a night a the museum, you'd be sitting in front of it all night
( ) You have no favorite

Did you ever buy a piece of art?
( ) Not yet   ( ) Yes, in fact you did
( ) No, you wouldn't pay for art

You like art
( ) ever since you were born.
( ) because your parents like art.
( ) because your friends like art.

( ) You don't know much about art, to be frank.

People who don't care about art
( ) are so uncultured.
( ) are relaxed.

( ) are *(adjective)* _____

A living artist you would like to meet:

(this artist) _____

A dead artist you would have liked to hang out with:

(this artist) _____

If you were an artist you would most likely do
( ) sculptures.
( ) paintings.
( ) photography.
( ) video.
( ) performance art.

or

(this) _____

Your favorite art museum:

(name) _____

_____

Your favorite art gallery:

(name) _____

_____

10 Things making you happy just by looking at them

1) _____

2) _____

3) _____

4) _____

5) _____

6) _____

7) _____

8) _____

9) _____

10) _____

What you like to listen to

Music

Your all-time Top 3:

1.
(song) _____

by (artist / band) _____

2.
(song) _____

by (artist / band) _____

3.
(song) _____

by (artist / band) _____

The music of your childhood:

_____

_____

_____

As a baby you were a rattle virtuoso.
( ) Yes   ( ) No

Today you think that you have a somewhat great singing voice.
( ) Yes   ( ) No

The first piece of music you bought with your own money:

(album) _____

(artist / band) _____

in (year) _____

( ) It was a CD
( ) It was vinyl
( ) It was a cassette
( ) It was a download

Right now you like to listen to

(artist / band) _____

( ) Makes you wanna dance   ( ) Makes you wanna sing

Music is something you like
( ) to make.   ( ) to listen to.

You wouldn't admit publicly that you like this song:

(song) _____

by (artist / band) _____

This friend has an incredible taste in music:

(this friend) _____

Music for every mood:

When you feel *(fill in each)*

happy, you play *(this artist)* _____

the blues, you play *(this song)* _____

in love, you play *(this artist)* _____

angry, you play *(this song)* _____

like running, you play *(this artist)* _____

like singing, you play *(this song)* _____

like dancing, you play *(this artist)* _____

tired, you play *(this song)* _____

like going to sleep, you play *(this artist)* _____

Musically speaking you would have loved to live in this era:

(era) _____

Your favorite online music platform:

www. _____

Let's get physical

Sports

Your favorite sport

to watch *(this)* _____

to play / exercise *(this)* _____

( ) You watch sports, you don't do sports
( ) You do sports, you don't watch sports
( ) You do both
( ) You are against physical activity for personal reasons

As a child:

Your favorite athlete was

(name) _____

Your favorite team was

(name) _____

Your parents tried to encourage you to play
( ) soccer.
( ) basketball.
( ) tennis.
( ) golf.
( ) football.
( ) rugby.
( ) video games.
( ) by yourself.

Your favorite summer sport:

(this sport) _____

Your favorite winter sport:

(this sport) _____

You dreamed of becoming a superstar in this sport:

(this sport) _____

Your MVP this year:

(name) _____

(team) _____

You exercise
( ) once a month.
( ) once a week.
( ) once a day.
( ) not enough.
( ) too much.
( ) never ever.

Who do you shower with adulation?
( ) Your team   ( ) Your favorite player   ( ) Your coach
( ) Your mom

People

Who's your favorite person in the whole wide world?

(name) _____

(last name) _____

Your best friend as a child:

(name) _____

(last name) _____

Your best friend today:

(name) _____

(last name) _____

You are most influenced by

(name) _____

(last name) _____

You are a people person.
( ) Yes, people are your kind of people.
( ) You are somewhat selective.
( ) People think you are socially awkward
( ) You are a hugger.

( ) You are more of an animal person.

What you like to watch

Movies & TV

Your 3 all-time favorite movies:

1. *(movie)* _____

2. *(movie)* _____

3. *(movie)* _____

Your favorite TV-show right now:

(title) _____

on *(channel)* _____

The first movie you went to see in a theatre:

(this movie) _____

Your favorite TV show as child:

(title) _____

Your parents enjoyed watching
( ) the news.
( ) boring documentaries.
( ) superfluous political talks.

You discovered the Discovery Channel at

(this age) _____

Your parents let you watch TV *(choose two)*
( ) to shut you up.   ( ) to be able to sleep in.
( ) to get stuff done.

The last movie you watched and liked was

(this) _____

A TV show that should go on forever:

(title) _____

Which one is it?
( ) You used to watch too much TV   ( ) You watch too much TV
( ) You watch too little quality TV

You prefer watching movies *(choose as many as you like)*
( ) online by yourself.   ( ) on TV with others.
( ) at the drive-in theatre.   ( ) on a date.   ( ) on a plane.
( ) in a car.   ( ) with lots of noisy junk food.   ( ) late at night.
( ) on a rainy Sunday.

You wouldn't publicly admit that you like watching

(this TV-Show) _____

You would seriously consider breaking up if you found out
that your partner didn't like

(this movie) _____

Colors

Your favorite color as a child:

(color) _____

Your favorite color right now:

(color) _____

( ) It's still the same

A color you don't like:

(color) _____

Your favorite color combination:

(color 1) _____

and

(color 2) _____

A color your could wear almost every day:

(color) _____

You got this book in this color because
( ) it sticks out in your bookshelf.
( ) the person who got it for you doesn't know you
nor what you like.
( ) it's your favorite color.

Stand up for your ride

Transportation

Your favorite way to get from A to B:

(this) _____

As a child, you loved to travel by

(this) _____

You prefer
( ) public transportation.   ( ) private transportation.

You own
( ) a skateboard.
( ) a bicycle.
( ) a motorbike.
( ) a car.
( ) a boat.
( ) a plane.
( ) a horse.
( ) a ticket to ride.

You would love to be able to operate

(this vehicle) _____

_____

If money didn't matter, you would only travel by

(this) _____

What is your favorite car?

(brand / model) _____

(color) _____

Your preference:
( ) Driver seat   ( ) Shotgun!   ( ) Relaxing in the back

You like the photo on your driver's licence:
( ) Yes   ( ) No

You usually get your rental car from this company:

(this) _____

Your favorite bus line:

(this) _____

Your favorite subway stop:

(this) _____

Your favorite train station:

(this) _____

Which one is it?
( ) Self driving vs. ( ) Driving yourself
( ) Horsepower vs. ( ) Horse
( ) Ride sharing vs. ( ) Carpool

Your favorite airplane:

(this) _____

Your favorite airline:

(this) _____

Your favorite airport:

(this) _____

You like to move on water in
( ) a sailboat.   ( ) a motorboat.   ( ) a big ass yacht.
( ) a cruise ship.   ( ) a submarine.

or *(this)* _____

If you could time travel, you would

( ) go forward in time.   ( ) go back in time.
( ) stay right where you are.

Where you like to like

Online

Your favorite website at the moment:

www. _____

Your first favorite website (*if you can remember*):

www. _____

Your favorite mobile app:

(*app name*) _____

It's
( ) very useful.
( ) just for fun.
( ) app-solutely vital to you!

Your preferred social network:

(*name*) _____

Your daily dose:
( ) One hour a day
( ) More than two hours a day
( ) Less than you think
( ) Just enough to stay connected

The first person you added and liked on your favorite social network:

(*name*) _____

A person you unfriended lately:

(name) _____

Why? _____

_____

Of all your friends you like this person's posts best:

(name) _____

Because they are
( ) just so funny!   ( ) extremely inspirational.
( ) always cute little kittens!!!!!!   ( ) short and crisp.
( ) selfies of a cute face.   ( ) not selfies.
( ) making your day.

A hashtag you like to use right now:

_____

( ) You don't do hashtags - you do hashbrowns

You like the concept of online dating:
( ) Yes   ( ) No   ( ) Swipe right

In your social media profiles you like to appear
( ) younger.   ( ) bolder.   ( ) better looking.
( ) more successful.   ( ) just the way you are.

When you feel

social, you go to www. _____

anti-social, you go to www. _____

like shopping, you go to www. _____

flirtatious, you go to www. _____

bored, you go to www. _____

unloved, you go to www. _____

like likes, you go to www. _____

angry, you go to www. _____

sad, you go to www. _____

happy and fulfilled, you stay offline.
( ) Yes ( ) No

What you like to read

Books

What is your all-time favorite book?

(title) _____

_____

(author) _____

You
( ) read it all at once.
( ) read it when you were little.
( ) bought it because someone recommended it to you.
( ) had trouble coloring within the lines.

A book from your early childhood
which your mother or your father read to you:

(title) _____

_____

(author) _____

( ) It made you fall asleep ( ) It made your parents fall asleep

The first book you enjoyed reading on your own or with just a little help from your parents or siblings:

(title) _____

_____

(author) _____

Your favorite author at the moment:

(author) _____

In school you were considered a book worm.
( ) Yes, definitely! ( ) Haha, not at all!

You prefer reading your books
( ) the old fashioned way.
( ) on your tablet or smartphone.
( ) to your children.

A working title for the story of your life:

(title) _____

You admire people who read a lot.
( ) Yes ( ) No

Right now you are reading

(title) _____

(author) _____

( ) You can't put it down!
( ) You are reading it because it was recommended to you
( ) You will probably never finish it

You are a fast reader.
( ) Yes   ( ) No

Reading is something you
( ) don't really like.
( ) tolerate.
( ) are passionate about.

When you finish a book
( ) you keep it.
( ) you recycle it by giving it to a sibling or friend.
( ) you use it as paperweight.

The book you are holding in your hands is definitely becoming one of your all-time favorite books.
( ) Definitely

Happy Ending

Now that you reached the last page of this book:

You feel like getting

(this) _____

You feel like getting rid of

(this) _____

You feel like getting in touch with

(this person) _____

( ) You feel like getting online.

( ) You feel like staying offline.

What I Like made you (*check as many as you like*)
( ) think.
( ) wonder.
( ) happy.

Notes

www.ingramcontent.com/pod-product-compliance
Lightning Source LLC
Chambersburg PA
CBHW071145060526
44107CB00132B/224